W9-BCX-930

CPS-MORRILL SCHOOL LIBRARY

3 4880 0
H

531
LEP

C.1

3 4880 05001074 8
Lepora, Nathan.

High-speed thrills :
acceleration and
velocity

$13.56

DATE DUE	BORROWER'S NAME	ROOM NO.
12-10-09	Tamara Loy	
V-2-10	Diego Davila	
11-4-11	Luis Rodriguez	115
	Diego Davila	212
		209

531
LEP

3 4880 05001074 8
Lepora, Nathan.

High-speed thrills :
acceleration and
velocity

CPS-MORRILL SCHOOL LIBRARY
CHICAGO PUBLIC SCHOOLS
6011 S ROCKWELL ST
CHICAGO, IL 60629

449162 01356 39077B 41446E   0001

IGH-SPEED THRILLS

ACCELERATION AND VELOCITY

By Nathan Lepora

**Consultant: Suzy Gazlay, M.A.,
science curriculum resource teacher**

Gareth Stevens
Publishing

531
LEP c.l

2008
13.56

Please visit our web site at www.garethstevens.com.
For a free catalog describing our list of high-quality books, call 1-800-542-2595 (USA)
or 1-800-387-3178 (Canada). Our fax: 1-877-542-2596

Library of Congress Cataloging-in-Publication Data
Lepora, Nathan.
    High-speed thrills : acceleration and velocity / Nathan Lepora—North American edition.
      p. cm. – (The science behind thrill rides)
    Includes index.
    ISBN-13: 978-0-8368-8943-7   ISBN-10: 0-8368-8943-6 (lib. bdg.)
    ISBN-13: 978-0-8368-8948-2   ISBN-10: 0-8368-8948-7 (softcover)
    1. Speed—Juvenile literature. 2. Acceleration (Mechanics)—Juvenile
literature. I. Title.
    QC137.52.L47   2008
    531'.112—dc22   2007042000

This North American edition first published in 2008 by
Gareth Stevens Publishing
A Weekly Reader® Company
1 Reader's Digest Road
Pleasantville, NY 10570-7000 USA

This U.S. edition copyright © 2008 by Gareth Stevens, Inc. Original edition copyright © 2007 by ticktock Media Ltd.
First published in Great Britain in 2007 by ticktock Media Ltd., Unit 2, Orchard Business Centre, North Farm Road,
Tunbridge Wells, Kent, TN2 3XF United Kingdom

ticktock Project Editor: Sophie Furse
ticktock Picture Researcher: Lizzie Knowles
ticktock Project Designer: Emma Randall and Hayley Terry
With thanks to: Carol Ryback, Justin Spain, and Suzy Gazlay

Gareth Stevens Creative Director: Lisa Donovan
Gareth Stevens Graphic Designer: Farimah Toosi
Gareth Stevens Cover Designer: Yin Ling Wong
With thanks to: Jackie Glassman and Jayne Keedle

Picture credits (t = top; b = bottom; c = center; l = left; r = right): Alamy: 18. Richard Bannister: 21. Cedar Point: 17t,
25. Corbis: 15b, 23b. Lester Lefkowitz/Getty Images: cover. Photolibrary/Digital Vision: title page, 4–5. Joel Rogers: 1
14. Shutterstock: contents page, 16–17, 20b. Courtesy of Six Flags Great Adventure: 9. Courtesy of Six Flags Over
Georgia: 10. Illustrations by Justin Spain: 6–7, 11b, 12b, 13 inset, 22b. Superstock: 22–23, 26–27, 29. Illustrations by
Hayley Terry: 8, 19 all, 24, 28c, 29c. ticktock media archive: 7tr.

Every effort has been made to trace copyright holders, and we apologize in advance for any omissions. We would be
pleased to insert the appropriate acknowledgments in any subsequent edition of this publication.

All rights reserved. No part of this book may be reproduced, stored in a retrieval system, or transmitted in any form c
by any means, electronic, mechanical, photocopying, recording, or otherwise, without the prior written permission of
the copyright holder.

Printed in the United States of America

1 2 3 4 5 6 7 8 9 10 09 08 07

CONTENTS

CHAPTER 1: FORCE

What makes roller coasters so much fun? Maybe it's that feeling of your stomach floating up inside of you. That feeling is caused by forces. **Forces** are the pushes or pulls that change an object's **speed** or direction.

THE FUN OF PUSHES AND PULLS

The basic design of a roller coaster is simple. Riders sit in cars that roll along fixed tracks. Unlike regular cars, roller coasters cars don't have motors. Instead, they rely on natural forces to propel them as they swoop and swerve along the tracks.

Different forces act on the car as it drops, turns, and loops upside-down. Forces push the car along the tracks at high speeds. Other forces try to slow it down. Forces prevent the car from flying off the tracks.

Forces also act on the people inside the cars. As the cars twist and turn, different forces push and pull the riders. Forces make riders hold on tight and scream in excitement!

THAT'S AMAZING!

The most exciting roller coasters can make you feel as if four people are sitting on you!

KNOW YOUR FORCES

Forces cause a change in shape, speed, or direction. Many forces combine to help make a roller coaster ride an exciting experience.

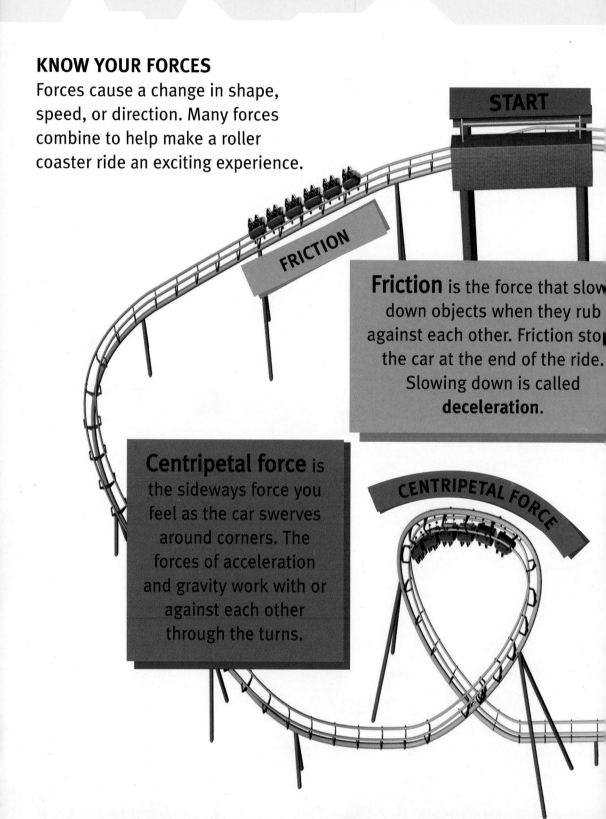

START

FRICTION

Friction is the force that slow down objects when they rub against each other. Friction stop the car at the end of the ride. Slowing down is called **deceleration.**

Centripetal force is the sideways force you feel as the car swerves around corners. The forces of acceleration and gravity work with or against each other through the turns.

CENTRIPETAL FORCE

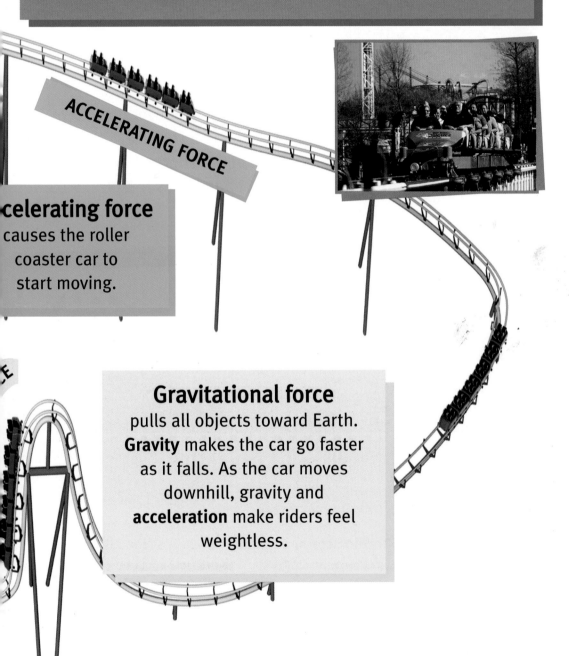

Inertia is not a force, but it is an important part of how objects move. Inertia keeps the car moving along its path unless a force acts on it to change its speed or direction.

ACCELERATING FORCE

...celerating force ...causes the roller coaster car to start moving.

Gravitational force pulls all objects toward Earth. **Gravity** makes the car go faster as it falls. As the car moves downhill, gravity and **acceleration** make riders feel weightless.

CHAPTER 2: SPEED AND VELOCITY

On a roller coaster, the world whooshes past as you speed along the tracks. Speed is how fast an object moves. Two factors determine speed: the distance an object travels and the time it takes to travel that distance.

SPEED AND DISTANCE

Faster objects travel farther than slower objects within the same time period. Think of a car race. The drivers try travel the same distance in the shortest amount of time. The car with the greatest speed wins the race. We often measure speed in miles per hour.

50 miles (80 kilometers) per hour   60 miles (100 kilometers) per ho

Speed is not just about moving fast. Every moving object has a speed, no matter how slowly it moves. Even the slowest snail has a speed.

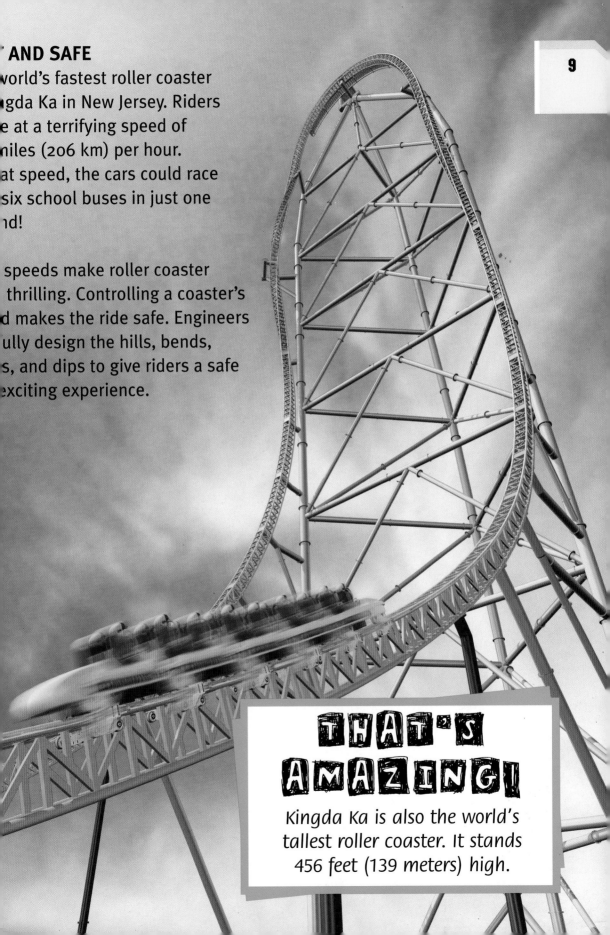

AND SAFE

world's fastest roller coaster
gda Ka in New Jersey. Riders
e at a terrifying speed of
miles (206 km) per hour.
at speed, the cars could race
six school buses in just one
d!

speeds make roller coaster
thrilling. Controlling a coaster's
d makes the ride safe. Engineers
ully design the hills, bends,
s, and dips to give riders a safe
exciting experience.

THAT'S AMAZING!

Kingda Ka is also the world's
tallest roller coaster. It stands
456 feet (139 meters) high.

WHAT IS VELOCITY?

On a roller coaster, speed can give you plenty of thrills. But **velocity** is what really makes your heart pound.

SPEED VERSUS VELOCITY

It's easy to confuse speed and velocity. Speed is simply a rate of movement. Velocity is a measure of speed *and* direction. A coaster racing down a hill might have a speed of 60 miles (100 km) per hour. Its velocity would be 60 miles per hour *downward*.

When a roller coaster track bends in a different direction, the car's velocity changes. It makes the world spin in exciting ways.

curve on the Goliath
aster in Georgia is part
hrill. The car's velocity
as it rounds the bend.

Zooming along a turn on a roller coaster shows how speed and velocity differ. The car's speed stays the same while swerving through the turn. Its velocity, however, changes quickly through each part of the turn.

CHANGING VELOCITY

Imagine velocity as a pointing arrow. The arrow shows the direction in which the car is moving. Whenever the car moves in a new direction, its velocity changes. The arrow shows how it changes by pointing in the new direction.

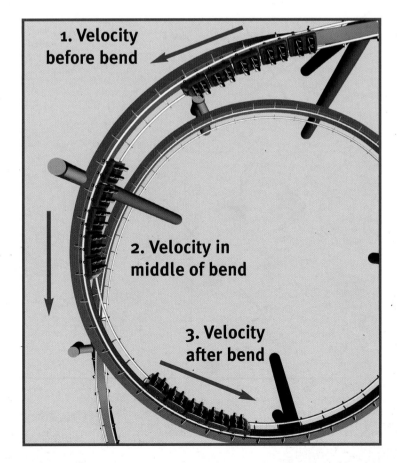

1. Velocity before bend

2. Velocity in middle of bend

3. Velocity after bend

CHAPTER 3: ACCELERATION

On a good roller coaster, velocity is always changing. Some of the changes happen slowly, such as the slow climb up the first hill. Most happen in the blink of an eye: a quick loo or a sudden turn. The rate at which velocity changes is called acceleration.

HOW ROLLER COASTERS ACCELERATE

The hills on a roller coaster affect acceleration. A car accelerates as it zooms down a hill. As it climbs the next hill, the car's velocity decreases. This change is called **deceleration**.

Designers carefully plan roller coasters. They place the hills at certain spots to control acceleration throughout the ride. The height and the number of hills has a big effect on acceleration.

THAT'S AMAZING!

Remember: Acceleration is a change in speed or direction. So a coaster that is zipping straight ahead at a constant speed has an acceleration of zero!

BOOMERANG ROLLER COASTERS

One type of roller coaster is called a boomerang. A cable pulls the car to the top of a very steep tower. Riders stare straight down at the ground hundreds of feet below.

The car is released and accelerates quickly down the slope. Riders hang on tight as the car swoops through two huge turns and a giant loop. The car decelerates as it climbs a second tall tower. It slows to a stop at the top of the tower.

Riders breathe a sigh of relief as they stare straight up at the sky. But the ride is not over. After a split second, the car rolls backward down the tower! The whole ride flashes past riders as they rocket back to the starting point.

Déjà Vu is a giant boomerang roller coaster in Atlanta, Georgia.

WHICH IS THE FASTEST?

It's easy to spot the fastest roller coaster at a theme park—just look up! The tallest roller coaster usually reaches the greatest speeds. Taller hills mean greater acceleration.

This is why the first hill on a roller coaster is usually the tallest. The speed the car gains as it roars down the hill is enough to propel it through the rest of the ride.

The stomach-churning drop Dodonpa, a roller coaster Fujiyoshida, Japan, is shown here.

THAT'S AMAZING!

Dodonpa takes off as fast as a jet fighter. In fact, aircraft carriers also use catapults to launch jet planes.

PULT LAUNCHES

roller coasters have a chain that pulls the car to the top of the first hill. there, acceleration and gravity do the rest.

coasters use a **catapult** to provide an accelerating force. A catapult is ice that shoots a ride forward from the start. Dodonpa is a catapult er in Japan. It accelerates faster than any other roller coaster on Earth. ar reaches 107 miles (172 km) per hour in under 2 seconds!

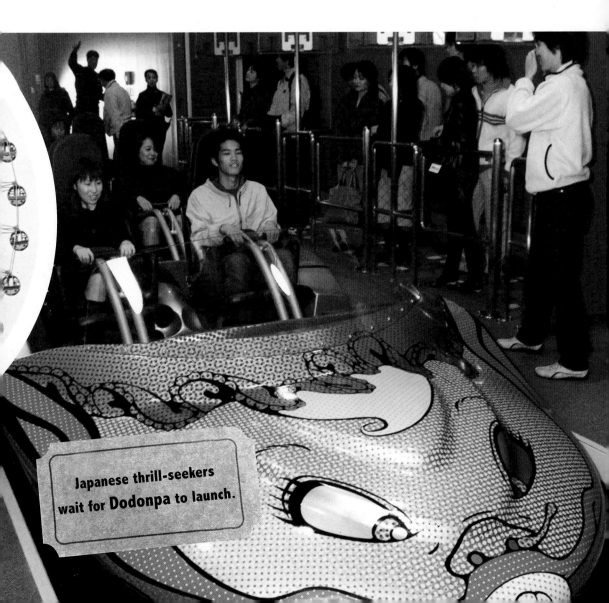

Japanese thrill-seekers wait for **Dodonpa** to launch.

CHAPTER 4: MASS AND INERTIA

It takes force to launch a roller coaster car. Some roller coasters use chain lifts to tow the cars to the top of the first hill. Other coasters use a catapult to launch the car. Heavier cars take more force to launch. That's because they have a greater **mass.**

WHAT IS MASS?

Mass is the amount of **matter** in an object. Mass makes objects difficult to move or to stop. Two objects of the same size can have different masses. You could probably throw a hollow plastic ball pretty far. It would be much harder to throw a lead ball of the same size. That's because the lead ball has a greater mass.

THAT'S AMAZING!

Even when empty, a train of six cars can have the same mass as an elephant.

WHAT IS INERTIA?

Like any object, a bumper car will stay still until a force makes it move. Once in motion, the car will drive in a straight line until you turn the steering wheel or another bumper car hits you! The tendency of an object to resist a change in motion is called **inertia.** It takes force to overcome inertia and make an object move, accelerate, or stop. Objects with greater mass have greater inertia. That means they require even more force to start, stop, or change direction.

ENTUM

ject's **momentum** depends on
ass and velocity. Imagine two
er cars traveling at the same
d. One car has two adult
engers. The other is driven by
mall child. The car with the two
adults has a greater mass, so
more momentum. It would be
r to stop.

would happen if you crashed
bumper car into the one driven
o larger adults? Since the
have more mass, their car
as greater inertia. Their car
take more force to move than
. Your car would probably just
ce off theirs.

a and momentum are what
s bumper cars so much fun.
ave to crash very hard into
er bumper car to knock it out
way!

BEFORE COLLISION

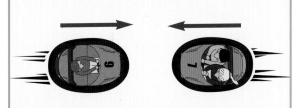

Cars 6 and 7 are moving at the same speed. Car 7 has greater mass because it holds two riders.

COLLISION

The cars crash straight on. The greater inertia of Car 7 causes Car 6 to change direction.

AFTER COLLISION

The momentum of both cars changes. Car 7 continues to move forward a little. Car 6 gets pushed back a lot.

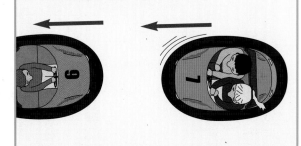

CHAPTER 5: WHEELS AND TRACKS

Roller coaster cars travel on wheels that roll over metal tracks. The tracks guide the cars.

OLD-FASHIONED ROLLER COASTERS

Old roller coasters are like trains. The cars ride on groove wheels that fit onto two metal rails. The first roller coaste ride in the United States, in fact, was built to be a railroa In 1829, Josiah White built a rail line with cars to carry co down a mountain in Mauch Chunk, Philadelphia. Before long, people started taking joy rides down the hill.

Old-fashioned roller coasters have wooden frames. Some people prefer wooden roller coasters because the wood makes the cars sway more than today's steel frames do.

The swaying of the tracks helps to absorb the force of the cars traveling over it.

MODERN ROLLER COASTERS

Most modern coasters are high-tech structures made of curved steel. The tracks are steel tubes that twist the ride through amazing turns.

THAT'S AMAZING!

The first roller coasters were ice slides. These were very popular in Russia in the 17th century.

The twists and turns of the **Superman Krypton** roller coaster at Six Flags Fiesta, Texas, are all part of the fun.

CHAPTER 6: FRICTION

Roller coasters can send riders zooming around at 70 miles per hour or more. So it takes a lot of force to stop them. **Friction** slows coaster cars down. Friction is a force that resist movement.

FRICTIONAL FORCE
When two surfaces rub together, they don't slide smooth Even surfaces that look smooth have tiny ridges. Those ridges catch and bump as surfaces slip against each othe The rubbing creates friction. That force works to slow the movement down. The rougher the surface, the greater the friction will be.

EFFECTS OF FRICTION
Friction is always at work between the tracks and wheels of a roller coaster car. That force slows and stops the train.

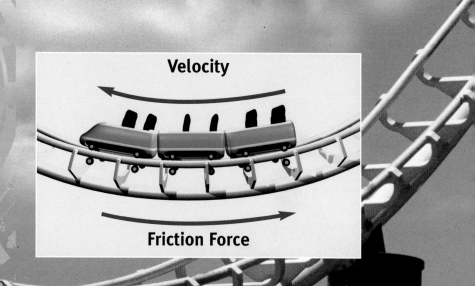

Velocity

Friction Force

Maglev trains can reach speeds of 361 mph (581 km/h).

MAGNETIC TRAINS

The Japanese **maglev train** uses **magnetism** to hover above the track. Because the train doesn't touch the tracks, there is very little friction. That allows the train to go very fast. Maglev trains are the fastest in the world. In the future, roller coasters might copy this design. That would make the ride much smoother, and even faster!

SMOOTH RIDE

Friction is important because it helps stop a roller coaster ride. Still, faster rides are more thrilling. That's why roller coaster designers have also found ways make the ride quick and smooth. They design the wheels and tracks t cause less friction as the cars roll along.

GUIDING AROUND TURNS

Most roller coasters have three types of wheels. Each type does a different job. Running wheels roll along on top of the tracks. Upstop wheels fit belov the tracks. Those keep the cars from flying off the tracks. Guide wheels run against the sides of the tracks. Guide wheels take over during turns to smooth the ride and cause less friction.

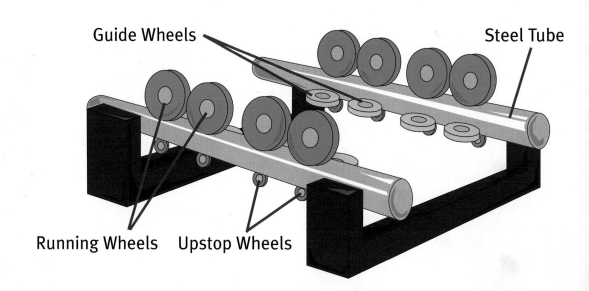

Guide Wheels   Steel Tube

Running Wheels   Upstop Wheels

SUPER-SMOOTH WHEELS

New roller coasters have wheels coated in high-tech plastics.
This covering makes the wheels much smoother than if they were just meta
The coated wheels quietly glide over the tracks to reach super-fast speeds.

TUBULAR TRACKS

Modern roller coasters run on special tracks made from steel tubes. The steel tubes are very smooth. They cause less friction, so the ride goes faster.

CHAPTER 7: AIR RESISTANCE

ir rushes past you when you ride on a roller coaster. This rush of air also slows down the car. **Air resistance** is friction between air and an object. Air pushes against moving objects to slow them down.

PUSHY AIR

On a windy day, you feel air pushing against you. Air is made of billions of tiny particles that bump into you. The wind pushing against you can make it hard to walk forward. The wind at your back, though, pushes you forward.

T FOR SPEED

rcraft and race cars have smooth, pointed shapes to help
move faster. Air rushes past them without causing much
on. The fastest roller coasters also have sleek designs to
e air resistance. Their front cars are shaped to cut through
he cars are also designed to protect people from tornado-
winds created by the speeding ride.

THAT'S AMAZING!

Parachutes glide slowly and
gently to Earth because
of air resistance.

CHAPTER 8: BRAKING

Like all wheeled vehicles, roller coasters ne[ed] a way to stop. **Brakes** are devices that use friction to slow something down. Most brakes a[re] like a sort of clamp that fits onto a wheel. Whe[n] you tighten the brake, it rubs against the whee[l] cause friction.

SLAM ON THE BRAKES

Roller coaster cars do not have brakes. There's no need t[o] panic, though. The brakes are built into the tracks. They clamp onto metal fins that hang beneath the cars.

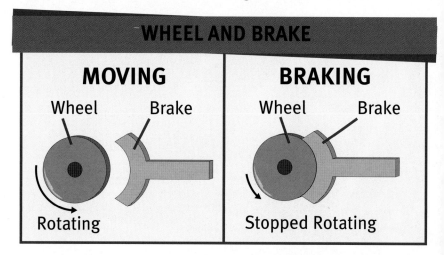

WHEEL AND BRAKE

MOVING
Wheel   Brake
Rotating

BRAKING
Wheel   Brake
Stopped Rotating

THAT'S AMAZING!

Friction brakes can be less reliable in the rain. Wet surfaces are slicker, so they create less friction.

STOPPING ROLLER COASTERS

Not all brakes use rough clamps. Air resistance is used for braking on airplanes. Flaps lift up on the wings to provide friction against air. Some newer roller coasters use magnetic brakes. These don't use friction at all. The metal fin passes between rows of **magnets** on the track. The magnetic force pulls the cars to a stop.

Brakes add to the fun of a roller coaster. They bring the ride to a screeching halt as a roller coaster ride ends!

ROLLER COASTER BRAKE

MOVING

BRAKING

SCREECH!

Fin

Brake

Fin

Brake

GLOSSARY

acceleration: a change in speed or direction; an object speeding up is said to accelerate

air resistance: friction between an object and air

boomerang roller coasters: roller coasters designed to return to the start by rolling backward halfway through the ride

brakes: devices that are purposely used to create friction to slow or stop an object

catapult: a device that throws an object in a certain direction at high speed. Catapults launch a roller coaster ride from its starting point

centripetal force: force that pulls an object toward the center as it travels in a circle

deceleration: a decrease in speed over time; the opposit of acceleration

forces: a push or pull that changes the shape, speed, or direction of an object

friction: force that slows or resists movement. Rough surfaces cause higher amounts of friction than smooth surfaces.

gravity: the force of attraction between objects. Gravity pulls objects toward Earth.

ia: the tendency of an object to maintain its speed, if that speed is zero. The inertia of an object is ed by its mass.

lev trains: trains that use magnetic force to levitate at above their tracks

netism: a natural force found in some metals, as iron. The force can pull metal objects toward each or push them apart.

nets: metals that attract other metals; usually those contain iron

s: how much substance something contains. Mass es an object to resist acceleration.

er: anything that has mass and takes up space

nentum: an object's momentum is its mass plied by its velocity. An object with a lot of entum is hard to stop.

d: how fast an object moves

city: a measure of an object's speed in a particular tion

INDEX